SLEEPING LATE
ON JUDGMENT DAY

SLEEPING LATE
ON JUDGMENT DAY

JANE MAYHALL

Alfred A. Knopf   New York   2004

THIS IS A BORZOI BOOK
PUBLISHED BY ALFRED A. KNOPF

www.randomhouse.com/knopf/poetry

Knopf, Borzoi Books and the colophon are registered trade-
marks of Random House, Inc.

The author wishes to thank the periodicals where some of
these poems first appeared: *Cedar Hill Review* ("The Tides of
André Gide"), *Commonweal* ("The Guess"), *Confrontation*
("The Conrad Aiken Dream," "Notes for a Sixtieth Wedding
Anniversary"), *The Hudson Review* ("The Forbidden,"
"Serenade"), *Louisville Review* ("Protection [Elegy for James
Still]," "The Shelter," "Wendell and Schubert"), *The New
Yorker* ("Token," "Why a Corner in the Apartment Puts Me to
Sleep," "The Comb"), *The Paris Review* ("Kirstein's Table"),
The Southwest Review ("Spending the Unspent"), *The Yale
Review* ("Uncensored Note to Auden").

Library of Congress Cataloging-in-Publication Data
Mayhall, Jane.
    Sleeping late on judgment day : poems / by Jane Mayhall.—
1st ed.
        p.   cm.
    ISBN 1-4000-4174-0
        I. Title.
PS3563.A96S58 2004
811'.54—dc21
                                                2003056180

Manufactured in the United States of America
First Edition

For Leslie George Katz

CONTENTS

I. Healing and Light

I

HEALING
AND LIGHT

TOO MUCH IS NOT ENOUGH

My heart is bursting with homage as I
head off to a hostile eternity,
pitiful thundering praises, the personal
of what I learned, individual lamps
conferred on the world's dark, the names
of my teachers, with quotes.

The worth vendors, their art and energy
drips with blood, in squalid abandon, never
or nearly in the best neighborhoods, their
books, and architecture, philosophy,
language, heroes of my

childhood's first punctured read.
I offer, offer—no piddle gratitude is
sufficient, a last designation
on suppliant knees, baskets of humility like ripe
grapes in the sun, my

desire to acclaim, at the height
of their never wane. Mysterious, like
painterly, my laconic lacerate and in vain
emptiness, where shall my hobbled, vigorous dreams
and voices go?

UNCENSORED NOTE TO AUDEN

To bask in your intelligence, when the wither
and time-gaps are stalking around me,
when the literal husks and brains never tried are
going to steer me off the road, I service
myself to the faint yellowed pages of this book, its
tiny lighted torch figure,

the running insignia on the spine of
a 1958 Modern Library edition, and I come to whatever dense
trilogies; compassion, spirited wit, wide-reaching
intellect, emotional power. These obviously
unstable and ridiculous concepts given
over to donkeys ("some great

gross braying"), predicaments out of date—in these
I would take long breaths of pure joy. The madrigal sunlight,
robust willows of your radiant, asymmetrical
and radically moral scorekeeping. The dreamy
semen of a distinguished flotsam. I need
that satirical pastiche,

against the false simplicity
your imitators have become.
The wrinkled Grand Canyon of your face gives me that
wreath, infinitude; the tropics and winter of
the real world you have reproachfully
left us.

SPENDING THE UNSPENT

Jerking alive, there is temerity in
the spasm. Easy does it.

Understand the goodness in moving. A horse
shakes its flank to rid the fly;

dog's ears waggle, a distant whistle;
rise to the occasion.

Waiting in her satin shoe, the Dancer feels
the indrawn muscle extend, foot

inclined to punctuate and taper.
In the continuing of the Soul,

eruption from the crater—compassion as from
the orifice of a volcano, flickering

neighboring signals. Out of
our unspent isolation.

TOKEN

In the bottom of my shoulder bag
I found a subway token from about eight tokens
back, that makes it long ago,
a monumental oldie. What's it made of?
Bronze-copper beveled and a dull sterling inside glow.
The "NYC" insignia like a secret fraternity embellish.
Brings to mind! Lively morning stench,
hot steel rails, the crowds
I used to sink in.

I could get up and down subway steps, I wasn't
dying. I loved dirt and torn-up newspapers, I was
able to walk. I wrote, it was like a church, like a god-
less tabernacle was God. That was
young. Whirling past the Coney Island darkness,
into flared faces on the platform, the token
rides my hand in the crush.

The old New York system. I remember
a black guy in a baseball cap, two legs gone, coming
through aisles, on a platform on skate wheels,
dignified and with a beautiful
voice. People dropped quarters and tokens
in his basket. He wasn't sanctimonious or drugged on
crime, or we didn't know it.

A token of the incommensurate.
(Even if wrong) I wasn't dying then and could
afford to think in
big words.

IN NEW YORK

Irritability is patience,
cynicism is wonder,
ambulance is gridlock,
up is up, down is
up, loud is fun.
Confusion is maneuver,
sunset windows are
like dappled apples—
true love is good weather;
faith, a soundless
tugboat on the East River.

THE APPLE ACCIDENT

A windstorm knocked all the apples down,
the ripe sheen had been perfect,
rose-tinted and sleeping in their shapes under
the faintly golden-green autumnal leaves.
Before the apple harvesting, wrapped each in a light
of expectation.

Then, the wind's abnormal blasting, unflattering
lances of hurled attack armies,
gusts that twisted the beautiful little
stunted gnome-trees, till they bled the bonny fruits;
icy hail and tornado rubbish hitting
and the dark rain;

and apples came to ground. They weren't dead,
only bruised, firm-skinned and warm
with all latent delicate flavors. Just rolled to a stop.
But ruined for commercial purposes, the crop was
a failure. And thrown into disgusting vats, not even
for cider or applesauce.

Along with nature's destruct, they'd have come
to nothing anyway. You can think of a million other freak
examples, of shock, malicious degradation, shamed
garbage. But to explain these apples flocked in orchards, their
sheen and rosy delight, was some height
of maturation, not that it's right.

THE WHITTLED FOREST

My father taught himself
to play the violin in
the pantry

with jellies and jams,
the garbage can and a broom. He
scraped the strings with

a stringed bow, the cold
curved wood in winter tucked
under his chin,

like the arc
of a whittled forest unknown.
It sounded awful.

He was a poor man
job-raising a family, struggling
with daybreak.

He worked at a night job
and practiced half the day on
scales. That is

why we mocked
his effort.

EXPERIENCE

As soon as you try to define,
it gets lost. If you
don't define, that gets lost too.
Smudging, rubbing, make the edges true.
You keep meeting the down-to-earth
denial that there is any value
or transcendence, only colors bouncing
against or together.

There must be something in rendering
the browns and blues and yellows of a rising
moon, in trying to silver how the water brims.
Happens of itself, the mirages of
distance and the arrival point
of love, marking passion with an honor, drawing
a responsibility like
Spinoza slivered the lens to
dock the light.

And you can't aim at loss either.
The one who brought the process almost nearest
was Wallace Stevens. And he kept his
office doors closed.

WASTEBASKETS

So not to make so many mistakes in
the eyes of others, I wanted to invent
a secret wastebasket, to throw away misleading
prattle, mountainous as survival,
disown what I said.

Pristine as snow, hurtful as chimes,
like a flowering theater party
asked only by God. A diminutive music box
that played a remembered poetry, my
errors and bright circulations.

But meant to be neat,
my imagined wrongdoing, into
some receptacle. Imagine a catharsis,
public statement improves, and
thoughts anew—in all that

heaven and debris, a lot of
my first gut ideas
were right.

RIGHTEOUSNESS IS KLEENEX

Righteousness is her Kleenex,
wipes away her tears,
spits the bloody rejects into
the layered soft.

Is virtue's fabrication,
a little dainty disposable she
snatches from the box. The thought
of being right absorbs

each smudgy doubt. And rubs out consequences
when mistakes have spattered life,
like the dirty works of god,
worse than lipstick

traces. It's so awful, superficial:
real virtue's out of step,
but pseudo keeps in time. For the anomalous
and disrelated, jack it

off. And swipe commitments
dumb. Sweet condescending attitudes,
like flowery-scented tissues, convenient
to most bathrooms.

THE CANE

This crevice where I put
my cane becomes a coastal harbor.
Shark-like enemies, gorging sea-lips may not
speak against those and that—
who kept me sane.

From the time of childhood's unbargaining
kindnesses, the comfort offered.
Like modern caves of Public School where I could
hide, to stave off mob justifications.
Now, after a life of skull & bones,
yet the reprieve.

Love's rigor held, little stubby sticks
potential as God. And I could find my way again.
In the bleak air, and know the place
to prop my cane. Self-help purloined, this
corner between adjacent walls,
to hoist me on.

2001, A BACKWARD GLANCE

Men are mad so unavoidably that not to be mad would
constitute one a madman of another order of madness.

—PASCAL

Busting out with mumble,
the year when low-grade virus opinion
took on hysterical prestige.
Inability the only right,

but technically perfect.
The year that turned to smirk,
and when music of a foul repetition
stacked the money.

Homer was not here, or Whitman—
who forgave even laundry lists, and was
quoted, "America, wake up!"
The classics of Western thought hid

from the public genre in bad remakes.
Cowardice, looting cowardice.
Jazz polarizing Mozart, when nobody needs
a divorce. Satire was limp

spaghetti. Computers were great,
but their side effects did
vital injuries. Like exiled Poles, a
few recited books,

a cataclysmic backward glance.
When arcs were built to
drown us.

THE TIDES OF ANDRÉ GIDE

On a tar roof in Greenwich Village
I read of Gide's death in the New York *Post,*
in 1951—the uniform soliloquies, the innocent shock,
like the unspoken lovers, husbands, brothers where
only touch was of avail.

Like a tidal river (memory was a factor) as
if the sweet bower of a college boy's kiss was related
to the far-fetched Gide, with his Algerian escapades,
and the long cape and French beret,
and my then illegible youth

sulking in the West Village.
I laved of him a rural poetry—in the New York *Post*
his aquiline vanished life weighed on me
mightily. Added the bus stop at
West Tenth and Bleecker tolled our intimacy.

He didn't represent a famous writer, but my affections
knotted close to the esteem of him.
Like the gray Manhattan pavement
underfoot. And was like some vague
friendship, forerunner of

grief. For on that day, I sighed for him.
And in everything I'd read, how
intensely personal was the universal.
Associations on the rise, from
my box on that

oily asphalt
roof.

SAY

Letting it have its say,
learning not to get
in the way. There's an old woman with
a face like paper clips, her carefully phrased Vienna accent,
memorizing the accent tutelage of hanging by (at Dachau)
her thumbs, the rest of her life,
justifying Hitler.
The jaded simple bait,

nobody has an ear for.
Letting the language in yourself be
attentive, and near enough to
be heard. Insulted or insulting—there's a
Jr. High student (American), his interminable loudness
like a big electric bulb.
Letting in the day, under the hard rain
of observation.

Planks across the brain
to keep from flooding, tides rise to
the same stages as your tears. I'm trying to turn
grief into madness and usefulness,
as if anything could ever again
be salvaged.

PROTECTION

Elegy for James Still

An evening ray in the shackles of mist,
your consciousness was my protection, the very
element of thought. Under your big straw hat, under
the doubt, companionate friends, springy inquisitiveness—
under the steady-eyed questioning, like a
farmer at work,

your interior vulnerability was my protection.
Of instant identity, the incommunicable
values. When you said to me when we were walking at
Hindman, "How can you stand to live away from the trees?,"
was it meant, their pride and accessibility?
You needed them, as people needed you.

All slowly vanishing from
the nature of gods and survival.
Like you once noticed in a busy town, a
thicket by the roadside. Or the first old house
you lived in, the pine wanderings and paths,
their hesitant certainties.

You are the stream that splashed
on my wrist, diverse, deep, the names of
things you named; bare truth like a shelter,
unflinchingly unresolved.
In Miltonian form, your shy abundance and disturbances.
Grace and virtue, readable

like grass, wind,
trees.

BRUEGHEL'S GAMES

I had to wait a whole life
to get the sight lines, the temperament
and birthright. Like at ten years old, practicing
tennis at dawn, the Public Park—I had to
wait the best period to
feel accustomed.

And all the swift emergency now
with old age, I had to wait the entire life
to smell the open road. Get a hand
on the rein and say I'm here.
Old age is like being
an emigrant,

the tincture of everlastingness
affecting vision and surmise.
And oh, beloved items departed! Now I
sit and tell, it's what
I know. The picture

has color and range.
And much like Brueghel the Elder's
representation of the exotic implements
of children's games they used to play,
their stocky little frames,

the short day's sport.

MY NEPHEW AND HIS WIFE

Some riders when they've done
with them, throw their horses away.
Who galloped the grassy sward, brisk on
a summer's day, buckles and saddles quoting
castanets in the sun.

My nephew and his wife, stern lovers
of the equine, when their gallants died,
buried them gently in the front yard.
But other amateur horse-trainers in Alabama
just canceled their *beau-cheval*,

once they'd either broken their
spirit, or let expire. And (incidentally,
against the law) carted sleek beauties
off to the dump. But my nephew
and his wife, crack riders

and young at heart, had a sense of
the morning light. And picked up their flickering
shovels. Like hooves clopping through
the dark, did their immortal,
solemn work.

PHOTOGRAPHER

This is the accuracy that is exhilaration,
unfiled tutors,
instancy of the poetic,
festival.

It is the common, unforced life; faces, shadows,
cars. Here in the city, a core-light
operating, as with music
or the sea.

A Shelley-like meditation,
introvert, finely spaced out. Because people . . .
and do they flow in a
parliament of

observation? In a tangle, and tangible
action. Like flowers they are,
in your department of
no resentment,

wrinkled or smooth.
Solitary is that kingdom,
garnet wheels of a
rich craving.

And your exact, private
intake is more true
than dreams. Because consciousness
is the dream.

HEALING AND LIGHT

Lying in wait, the undersoul,
when something hurts, you
can't heal it with descriptive passages
or wise-guy quips,

or human sacrifice. Like the satellite true
feature story on Rio de Janeiro and
the massacre of homeless children,
no double-talk.

Holding back the mismatch, misunderstanding
is the loneliest paradox, far-seeing
with only faith to build on—life's belittling
pathos, digging out.

When this lunar thing, notoriously
expired, in the swamp ditch of
the night, a moon of transfigured light
goes up, that would be dark

too, except filling the whole meadow,
so radiant, you could read
a newspaper by.

PICKING UP

Old man on Broadway walks down
busy street, edging at
the curb. Noncommittal, a
newspaper under one arm, he gets
joggled and drops the paper, and doesn't
notice. A young man sees

and rushes in, picks up the wadded
paper and says, "Hey!"
Old man jumps, covers his
body with two skinny hands, as if
to keep from being stabbed or
beat up. His face,

spotted with terror like
old age spots, spittled eyes gawking.
The young man says,
"You dropped your paper." The old man
writhes all in one place like
a sprint walker.

The young man wedges the newspaper
under the other's pipe-shaped
elbow. And walks off.
The old man lets go of his defending
manner and in a screech voice
yells, "Thanks, guy."

CRUDE THOUGHTS

It has to be new
             even if not true,
leaving out right
             it's got to be trite,
it has to be ugly
             with a soupçon of smugly.

It can't be loving
             without kicking and shoving,
and can't just feel good
             without buckets of blood,
and can't enjoy beauty
             without a sermon on duty.

Nor can inculcate self-doubt
             without a greedy pig-snout,
it can't help elder others
             without hating their mothers.
It can't rev a fast risky ride
             without the cult of suicide.

It can't ever be free
             without ceasing to be;
and yields not one iota pleasure or
             admits the obvious items that enliven
us, and crude thoughts to treasure and measure—
             that don't rhyme.

WISH FULFILLMENT

Wish fulfillment is the king
to the sere eyes of criminals,
or in the hackneyed kid-stuff lullabies,
a tippling so pure, we drink away
our lives,

having it all ways. Like the military paraders,
powerful-headed into death; in the unity
of suspended disbelief, even are the large coiffures of
little sexpots, clerks and secretaries
bobbing down Seventh Ave.,

anklets and bracelets on their skinny prime
meat, chattering at some heaven,
in large drafts of shop windows; no shop
talk, *oblivion*, to mar
their vision.

Strike while the iron is hot!
our delusion, in crests and spangles, as
fortified as jungle tribes;
clasped in their hands the amulets
of wishing.

From this perfection of thought
and happiness, come also architecture
and music, the beautiful stasis of what each
person desires. From our very
taste buds, to gods'

unverifiable
heapings.

WILLIAM STAFFORD,
COINCIDENT WITH EASTER

Just when I needed to read him, he
came again, the man who said:
"It's the poem that failed me that retains
my regard." The torn pages, deepest
confirmation, entered my pusillanimous debate.
Acorn of a system,

my rain-washed windowsill, where I could
look over into the forest I'll never enter; craft
and skill always falling into shadow. I am writing this
at Easter, when a William Stafford interview
from 1988, small press quarterly,
just fell off my

dusty shelf. Nothing that's not
related; how affix the mythos to the act? Stones rolled
away from the convicted failure—and into
articulation, unceasingly.
And that workshops
won't teach.

Receptivity wrote
the Bible, the ooze, begin
fathomless into . . .

UNACCOUNTABLY

A sentence from Spinoza, clean
and devious, made me remember about
when I first came to New York. Sitting in
a little park next to Christopher Street
in Greenwich Village, watching
traffic. His wisdom, humble to use; optician's vaulted
glass, and the Spinoza reincarnate abilities, made
a close association.

The subject and outer trappings not
related. But his language, viable to private threads,
ideas whisking through, unaccountably, when he
wrote, "Nature does not work with an end in view," was akin.
Witty, intransigent, a first elemental,
like black diesel smoking from a bus, and the limber
gird of leaves on a green and yellow
ginkgo in the park.

Was made to me evident,
the welling up of some mysterious similarity
in the book. Doors opened to a faculty of truth,
as close as the street, Seventh Avenue, in front of me.
Skeptical, not morbid. His vividness and concentration (like
a rumble of manhole covers) hauntingly
fresh. With a taste

of the ominous.
Litmus.

TO "EVEN"

To "even" is evening, putting it
straight. Also evening, a time between

dark and pale imbalance. And shards of
pink clouds, a star in its anti-gun holster,

ready to shoot beneficence to
everyone. And the light, fluffy

sundown going down with so much, I don't
want to even "even it up" (mountains

prying the vernacular) and don't want
to "get even." References to only

the vaguely discernible, as from the porch
of the avenue I lived on in a Southern

industrial town, and it "evened out" to
black. The faulty streetlight

ebb, like
honeysuckle.

SUN ON THE KITCHEN WALL

A bloom of light widening, grown as
from a corm, a lopped trunk of yellow. Not of
a crocus or gladiola, but close—new life,
an interior sunshine. And spreading to across the table

at a tomato in a wooden bowl.
The wafting intensity of every hue is bisected
into a double-red. And like shearing to
the very heart of the tomato, where ripped off the vine

is its dark leaf, soldier-suit green.
How far does the mind go swimming? why itemize?
except to steal virtue from the experience.
The sun fills the kitchen, succinct

as windowpanes, the mystery and hypothesis
come streaming from the sky into
the room. Not to be analyzed too much,
or purged into sainthood.

SOURCE BOOKS

My best friend Lucy, across the street, aged
fourteen when I was fourteen, said she "read at" a book
at night, to put herself to sleep.
The sight of printed pages made her legs go limp,
eyes flickered, a liquid malaise ran
through her physique.

Nothing about sex, but drugged on her resistance
to ideas, she was like a gelded dog.
Alert brain, silenced; books were the sleeping pills of
youth. Tho' funny papers entertaining, *Mary Worth*
and the Katzenjammers, but liable
to keep her up.

Her canny, homey escape-hatch was to slup away to bed
with *Silas Marner* and Ambrose Bierce, their
totem, unlikeable sentences, her antipathy made the blood pressure
decline. Into a coma went the mind—Lucy was that honest,
a sophisticated anti-intellectual at fourteen,
and I believed her,

but kept on reading. And courted lush insomnia of
a lifetime, worse than drink. In my staggered, imperative
convolutions, parked in the wilderness
of forever sleeplessness, I
didn't get a wink. While she snuggled, serene
across the street,

us, both conjured by the same causality
and logos, side by
side.

THE SNOW GOOSE

A half-empty cement bag, on the workers' trestle
suspended against a building across the street, fifteen
stories up, the bag looks like a winter snow goose.
Puffed-out breast, long slender neck
is the tough paper material, twisted for
closure. And at the top, a perfect, serene goose-
head, with almost a

beak. The illusion haunts for two days, even if
I've figured what it is. Could I shape my half-bag of words
into that sculptured deception? the next
morning, to be shook up, and used differently—I'd be
satisfied. The splattered innards,
cement and water, applied with a trowel, just
to repair a wall.

And the paper-gray, half-empty cement bag depleted,
destined for trash. My heart would still flip
to the mistaken, accidental first image. The winter-gray
snow goose, and its feathery lone-star
white breast, puffed up
with pride.

SHAPE OF SENTENCES

If they could just be a shape on a
page, and wouldn't hurt,
and wouldn't strive against inexact.
If they could lull by their
surreal fragments,
not real, but abstract—and that gets
better with time.

And drained of their belovedness,
to convey a completed thought.
Feel the rose colors, without the black,
sere separating that
words tell. Be like many a fine summer's day,
austere and life-

giving, paragraphs and sentences.
If I could just let them go
by, and not try to
hold them.

On the contrary, always apologize and explain,
in the terror-white veracity, down to the essence bone,
tenaciously follow the long road. Be
capable and Voltairean, discreet of form and substance, tell it
like it is, don't gloss over
in silent splendor.

Give the unattractive facts. But they won't be
that insipid (arrears of heavenly bodies).
And if you have to polish up
the contemptible gaff, give it all you've got—seriously,
don't swindle and pretend the sky
didn't fall in.

But dole out the mathematics, saviors of the gut.
Inching without propaganda the longhand
of dream. Even insult the host who
just wanted to play the game. Apologize in sample color,
if you loved something, say it. If kept
under your hat,

let the fallacies represent you.
From whatever Acropolis of stress, bat with
that genuine non-expurgation, the angel of bottomless pits.
Versatility and science; right the wrongs you know,
and do it with wholeheartedness. In fundamentals
so brash, or like a glass

of water.

MISS P

I've never known anybody more perfectly
without amend; more profoundly upright, not
judgmental, stray, not tame.
Wooly ski cap, on short gray hair,
gray and brown; like a compass, the blind asunder face
beneath it, the tumble of features adrift,
their perspicacity.

I had faith in the way she walked;
shuffling and limited. The gentle cruel look
of apology made me swear to proud distances;
a black string of melody followed every
joy. She was my neighbor every day on the elevator,
and seldom spoke but in a hushed
wisp of amusement.

I was created by the aluminum foil of
her sea blue eyes; teacher, old, abandoned, I
saw her climb the indecent sidewalks that, never causing
her to lie flat before them.
From the swim of New York, she loitered
between her apartment, and an
occasional bar.

Why did I love the battling tranquillity?
Today, I learned the answer;
after last week the Super found her in the kitchen
with all gas burners on. No flame; but in
her suffocation, she was resisting.
And she was resuscitated by Roosevelt Hospital medics,
and five days later, this afternoon,

I met her, careening up the street,
with a tallow eagerness, still at the smiling mouth.
And ski cap yet askew; I saw that defeat
for a moment was her courage.
I saw the misconstruction of all interpretation.
And no sculptured monument of her could
be anything but fledgling.

And no poem could teach the pain,
and the nothing that wouldn't save her;
yet crossed like serenity in
a bolt of lightning; and she turned a glance
toward me, and said, "How are you?
I've been away."

LISTENING AND HEEDING

The whinny of a horse
on Central Park West knocks out all artifice,
the accomplice to states of landscape.
Like my once familiar Kentucky back-alley, where
a rag picker's horse and wagon went by.
Not only a reminder, but a
species of distillation,
unlost memory.

It's like a piece of wood fallen off a house
where carpenters were building.
A child would understand the serendipity connection.
Like a storm on a seacoast, the choppy vista.
You get the pattern, the sequence of
anointing, knowing where you are
and what happened.

The voice of this New York carriage horse is of
the same sustaining. Against the fraudulent noisemaker city,
and even the viewpoint of most people,
who wouldn't hear the natural sound or pathos,
and the nearly insane grieving
of an animal. In their status denial,
nobody takes it on; or like

some dumb concession, the listening
and heeding.

LIKE OSCAR WILDE

He watches a thunderstorm outside,
leaning like Oscar Wilde at a full-length open window,
a wavered figure in white trousers
and an open-throat shirt.

What neighbors would see his melancholic stance,
a shadowy, unposed supplication, not merely
glancing outside his apartment, but
it's a giving of himself to

waves of thunder. The chances are nobody is
noticing, from the twenty-odd windows facing his
building. He is, in fact, concealed by
the covenant of rainfall;

a torso, unselfconscious, like a folded leaf.
And nobody can invade his imbibing posture,
refueled by this genesis—and I know
the idea sounds ridiculous.

Except, like a blast of lightning (I get from
the sidewise profile) he must have seen my
shadow, inappropriately also, leaning out in space.
And flings his window shut,
as if struck.

GLAD

I'm glad it does not quite work,
and does not include the stifling nearness
of a machine, or a critical authority breathing down
your neck. I'm glad it doesn't immediately suggest marriage,
and that Love that came from nowhere wasn't wearing
telescopes.

Eternity is the exhale of imperfection—that makes
the poetry of memory last forever.
I'm glad that striking a match may not light up
the world. Faintly near to wonder, God
won't tell where he's at. In jails of pure science, you
can't get out.

I'm glad of a street that holds our footsteps,
even at the price of non-decomposition. I'm glad that
William Blake doesn't make sense. And, of course,
because Death is the unacknowledged master of us all,
he still has to wait around while we
harmonize and protest

(like a little songbird's pretending).
Only in error's significant pause is there
maximum freedom. Trying to imagine everything
over again.

A DISTANT TRUMPET

Borne along humid winglets,
air for some reason from
a New Jersey source,
western to the West Side
on a veritable breeze
cogitating zephyrs.

Actually, it's the solo lead at
an outdoor jazz fest; early
noon at Lincoln Center
Plaza. High, offbeat
melancholy wafted;
not autumn but verging.

And a cool perpetuation of rich,
gold, and mellow. A musical
grasp on the stops like
Louis Armstrong, so classy
you can't figure how you can
even hear it at seven

blocks away. Tantalizingly un-
amplified. Improvised, we listen
to that single distant trumpet,
and for the rest of the day,
feel no pain. Riff
in the magnet skies.

DISOBEDIENCE

This tree did not know its named duties,
and when a June-like quest of
sunshine turned votive remark on unprepared branches,
its snow-borne senses to verdant green,
showers of pink apple blossoms
in the middle of January, pale red to rubaceous,
became the botanical foremen,
the saps of nature to

spring, it was the usual misnomer and infiltrations
that elude our usual pretend, our acceptance
of false schemes, where yet, what happens
in life and occasions opens
the universe to its many
evidences of opposite. Wherein ecstasy or pain
have taken over beyond the science of
books, computers, as on trees. Here in Central Park,

the showering pink apple blossoms
wackery, riverous, off-key, equivalent to
world change, wherein yearly or daily or
by the minute, we
never learn.

EMERGENCY ROOM ENJOYMENTS

Every relation is a flirtation, an
attraction of cheerful obedience or a
rejection. At New York hospitals, the savage
courtships run rampant, mostly on the indifference side.
When trained nurses have the best opportunity
for practicing the arts of mean treatments,
so clothed in
technological prowess, certificates
of experience and capability, the cold disguise
for punishment and destruction of what
they choose.

In the emergency room, there was
the case of an old shivering woman, brought
with rampant pneumonia, who was left for hours to shiver
and shake with paper towel covering her feet, while the nurses
in their crisp uniforms
exclaimed, she can't have a cover because we don't have
any, and the young physical therapist who brought
the old dame walked miles under the hospital to the basement
laundry where thousands of cozy warm blankets were warming,
and stole one to take back to the emergency room,
of morgue-like extensions,
to keep the dying woman slightly
presentable.

BALLAD OF PLAYING TENNIS WITH THEODORE ROETHKE AT YADDO

Noting his glowering blondness, I asked
him to play tennis, a midsummer hot
afternoon. He roused from the deep
of a king's ornate chair, a stirred gold
foliage of a man. The bulk of light heaviness arose,
and he said, "Sure?"

I said, "Sure," not knowing he was a
champion player, only the shadow beam poet,
from his father's dusky cellar.
On the dusty tennis court, the sweaty ambidextrous
swayed a disentangled gem; I caught the spirit
of graciousness that cut the air with
a kindly held-back serve.

Like quarks from some upper atmosphere,
he bore my insufficiencies with politeness
and forbearance. The intrepidity shone like
wine, as the slow heap of that
sprawled magnificence moved sedately.
Toxic and benign.

Like enchanted unmatched syllables, he
winged precise bemoan, gullible as
relinquished adversity. And pieces came together
in the unifying decree of
the hot melting
Yaddo sun.

OPINION

Life has pushed me into the escape-hatch
called Opinion, a refuge I hate.
Looking out at her troubling
unterritorial swashbuckle, how can
I reduce to the jaw-hinges
of saying what's right.

All in my safe little bunkers, not
all that safe. I notice it in bright companions,
the argumentative fealties
each a private jail. I want a vacation break,
the wanderlust of, say, Isaiah Berlin, opening
all the gates, with

the picklock of freed Opinion.
The runaway renegade, Robin Hood of going places:
determinate point of view, used indeterminately—
Ariel of deepest convictions, "lightly of
separation" (that's from Auden) tuned
to a stream of contradictions,
magnus of daily Need, more
like song.

KIRSTEIN'S TABLE

A conversation free of duplicity and
intellectual browbeat, as by wine unimpaired,
the intoxication ran high.
Demeanor and curiosity not prying—
was the clearest.

Manners like distilled waters from
a glacier and steamy hidden jungles, the white
and black lucidity passed around in cups.
Long moments brought silence that oddly resembled
the tablecloth, guests in

a kinship of guests.
Twenty years later, I dip bread in the freighted
wild pits (no man is a fable) and in
the clarity ritual of his every
night's last supper.

Words flowed from a grainy chair,
Lincoln Kirstein alluding to Don Quixote,
"truths are more beneficial than extravagances."
Nor kitsch nor melodrama, but very delicate stuff.
The unblemished unconventionality

rising from decanters of booze
and the frozen wonton soup thawing
out on our plates: perpetrators of the magic.
And himself in the background,
cordial, volatile.

THE FIRST DEATH

Was a horse, that ran out of an
alley onto Burnett Ave., in Louisville, Kentucky;

the alley bricks, mossed and russet.
He'd broke away from a coal wagon, the wild

eyes and foaming bridle,
and fell in the street, head landing

on the bricks. I was six, and thrust my own head
into a wedding of sensation, knowing

inescapably. The crowd gathering,
and its bloody appetite

hit me straight for the rest of
my life. The human lust for death

so grinningly expressed.
Many and many a funeral I have avoided,

for the dignity of the horse.
With his eyes wide open,

and our glances
meeting.

POSTCARD FROM A DREAM

God is the rim of my thought
to keep from explode,

is the treadmill of a load,
the Work under the road,

a made product out of air,
science of survival;

webbed dark opposed to the obvious
and given predatory delights.

Is our daemon of Constancy,
the slow recruits of choice, planting

music and incantation. But
the holiest things are seemingly inapplicable,

like a Bach partita, written for
strings, postcard from a dream,

the open, lush sound. With staff
and skein, the imaginary

boundaries, to break
the void.

WENDELL AND SCHUBERT

Flushed, he came home from the operetta
called *Blossom Time,* where at the Kentucky
Brown Hotel auditorium, he saw
the real Schubert in
velvet jacket

and armed with grace.
Flexed white fingers over a gold painted
piano, and the chorus sang like
pink roses, and saturated
with melody,

gave my brother's voice a rise.
And his own pink skin burned in ardors,
and tears stood in his kindled brown eyes, Wendell,
my brother, heard like bonfires he'd
never heard before,

in practicing and tedium, results.
And he was in love with Schubert
and allied, and the cardboard trees that stalked
the stage, and gave inspiration.
And he recited

to my mother and me the sage of Vienna
and the risk of art. And education
burst out of his closed-up American lips.
Wendell, already a grown-up working-class boy
(laugh, if you can)

and I was five. Never applicable
again, and I burned with him
on the stage of imitation
phony impressions like costume jewelry. And the composer's

life was rendered, so mistaken it wasn't even
sin. But Schubert's hidden voice soared
in the misapplication, by Wendell's
intake at the Brown Hotel,

his concentrated witness,
spirited and young.

YOUTH, AGE

On the plight of source material,
arrogant with certitude, I was at my
most effective. Now I've lost that charm that
glued the social lies, and spun my strong appeal.
The cool intent that patched and gave
the reliable sensation,

sunny grapes off center like shiny poems
falsifying what was real. The raw bunches of life,
yet unrevealed, I can't justify that I didn't
tell what was real, now doubt stands out.
When my crazy uncle aimed a gun at
the whole table of relatives, I had to

say, how quaint. My aunt talked him out
of it, the secret fact was her brave
act. At this unlucky stage of my
great age, I no longer want to cover up
the expanding text of unwelcome
truths—caught between the wrath of God
and unsure needs—that strike

the vain society as trivia. To
me, ornament to living, *Homo sapiens,* just in
time to see, the material sources—
distrusted, alert, unsure.
Scathing beautiful self-doubt,
traveling miles.

PRESUMPTIONS

A sixty-five-year-old poet writes
that he didn't know what he felt, as
atrocities were limping by, or
friends drank blue wine out
of pails of blue sky, I'm questioning
his veracity that he didn't know
the import.

When a sunlight's beam makes the square
window, over metal desk, show
the wood and glass to resemble a fuzzy halo,
it's a sensation of religious
awe. Not to repeat, without sounding foolish.
And memories! love's adult, pierced,
flesh-summoned Loss

sometimes terrorizing the entire room.
I feel it an invincible madness,
like a paint smear on happiness—the floor-
light rippling from the sun. These
unbridled emotions, I can't rub out by
saying I didn't know.

VESPER HOURS

End of long day suffering, from
the tips of chewed fingernails to the top
of her furrowed brow, beneath the scruffy clot,
dyed hair bangs, *chocolate kisses.* Eyes of a
child, batted against Mickey Mighty mall,
counters and aisles,

so much material, curtains, sweatshirts,
assassin dolls, as to make Zeus,
run screaming for that first birth, into the chaos
we all came from, and are bound for, she
lifts a stubbed hand and yells,
"Price check!"

From isles of negation, the cash box
like a spiritual retriever
in the assembly, she's a girl of twenty,
sacred as a cow, maybe mystic in how she stands,
at her post, waiting for the other clerk at
the back of the store

to bring the right tag from the housing
department. Like prayer beads,
inserts of credit cards into the machine. "What's
the percentage on the toaster?" "12.99."
Lips mumbling, inured to the wobbling
low moan air-conditioning,

taking comfort where we can.

THE CONRAD AIKEN DREAM

Last night I had a dream of Conrad Aiken, I hadn't seen him
in nearly thirty years, 1971, that's when
he died. In the concentrated privacy of the night he returned
as full as life, aslant on his old settee,
and was going to read his new poem on Li Po to my husband, Leslie,
and me, and his wife Mary. This was after the eleventh martini,
and the "plumblet" as he called his apartment on
East 33rd Street (there was a plumber's store on the first floor)
was quiet as a Christmas mouse in the intense, alcoholic
silence. Had happened pretty often, and now
it was a dream, and Conrad read eloquently, his
green Savannah eyes lifting from bifocals, to test our
great attention, which was habitually drunk (though
we used to pour a lot into Mary's flower pots when nobody looked)
and so the dream was excessive, with hot family-like
overtones, and we were dear friends.

And Li Po was wonderful, with Santayana and Christian Gauss
simmer at the roots, his (Conrad's) unsentimental
Harvard and other place teachers, so long ago, we all felt we
knew them well. And special Conrad!
still the child of murderer-suicide father, that had nothing
to do with my dream, and the mother his father killed.
Afterwards, years later at the assembly of a cemetery, in or near-
by, at which Conrad too died, following about a half-gallon of
vodka, he'd switched, I often thought of the little gold martini glass
in Spanish moss drapings; he used to have picnics beside
the grave and always poured a little bit at the end on the
headstones. He was indeed a lively tutor,
and in my dream I listened to the symphonic and manifest
friendship that held us all together, and realistically,
and not fame either. So what is this about?
My dream, pristine and unafraid. Leslie as calm as ever,
and Mary with movie-star brown eyes, nervously trying not to drink

too much, and myself without a shred of ambition, but
with a measureless affection nobody would believe,
and by now I'm not going to try to prove it, and the flourish
of the night! with leftover black olives
and carefully selected Irish salmon, and I can tell you there was
a security and trust worthy of Mount Vernon,
the Library of Congress, Winston Churchill and Robert Musil—
Conrad's name-droppings like old-fashioned chandeliers that lit
the brain, in that thrift-shop-furnished apartment, with
little crochet bargains Mary had found. Innocent!
and charming. And in my dream, because it was twenty-nine
years later, and I was almost as old as he was when he
died, and I bet that wasn't the reason after all, Conrad, finishing
his reading, leaned back and said, "Well, Jane, don't you
have a new poem somewhere?"
I said, making it up as I dreamed, you've got to remember, the words
came out of my dream, and not me, and I said, "Yes,
this is a poem called 'To My Favorite Poet,' "
I didn't know who I was talking about, phantasmal in the wings.
And in the moonlight of nowhere, and without moral
responsibility, and Conrad said, "Well, go ahead, Dearie!"
and I recited, "My favorite poet: he doesn't collect Oracles,
only Particles." Nobody said anything. I woke up.

VOICE

A boy telephoned, fifty years after
last she'd seen him at their hometown grocery.
Old man now, not the point. The boyish
velvety, retracted self-conscious
came to her like wine.
She gulped. "Hey,
Irving Nance!"

He gasped, that she remembered.
The chinked light of the old vegetable store
walked right out of the 'phone receiver,
his tormented, vague, brown-hewn eyes, had he been—?
(When terminologies are coroners
of rubbish.

Heterosexual is a dumb word too.)

"Well, durn you, Jane Mayhall,
you know who I was!"
Fifty years ago, she did. Only slightly.
But the prescribed, belated tonalities were stored
treasures, like blood cells' darkling wisdom
she'd kept. For what?

Nothing important,
just remembering a voice.
Their affectation flowed in tribute. His plane
heading back to Louisville was scheduled
for early next day. "So—
hello, goodbye."

II

LOVE POEMS

ALTAR

Imagine the books, the hallowed face
in a photograph. My dangerous crippled walk
to the font. I love the cloth covering
on the altar, the gold and crimson
square-shaped simplicity.

Ideas, like in a sequestered
tote bag. Under the pedestal are hidden
the work tools, screws and bolts,
and present for me, the lamp
burning on the life mask.

And holding up like a bookend, a
burly bee, that is a
sculptured frontispiece, for
an ancient car. It's the bond
of mystery.

Here sits all of my
steadfast companion,
Lost in the time warp
of another Day, always
with me.

THE RISK

All the lovers, denying, pretending
they didn't know what was
coming. I knew ahead I might lose you.
Your coat sleeve, presences, topography, pricked my
recognition, through soul, a
lost stability.

Path to light, that angles darkness,
our lying in the grass on a
mountain, hoisted biographies in the fragmented clouds
we watched, it was clear as the winds
that changed them. Face of
fate, that didn't

either have to be. Our incalculable
harmonies, bodies' lithe fabrication, seascape,
weather, mountains, the luck
whatever of place. Fulfillment swathed like
ammunition in the breeze,

your familiar warm shoulder, prescience—
so good there was nothing to say,
just the right pages turning,
beyond the storm, threat to our love,
their harbor risk.

NOTES FOR A SIXTIETH WEDDING ANNIVERSARY

Lofty, but not above it.
How could anything so rash happen?
The Baptist ice-cream, and a pitiful living room.
The Pastor in seersucker, red-faced,
bewildered as icons.

It was a wild decision, youth and Mercury
at our heels. The Parish didn't even have a piano.
But wedding strains, coached to overdo (and love
is private). The greatest concentration
was defiance.

Silence was the marriage ring we chose.
The cake I recall was Tastee brand,
you barely took my hand.
No urge for bridal costumes, heaven opening up
the purgatorial rites. And we

all stepped forth, in faith.
The worst disasters were golden givers of advice:
sausage makers. We liked to think of
living without a Name. And quandaries besmote—
like Oxymorons.

Because we didn't believe in obligations,
we never thought about divorce.
And we were blessed. Going to sleep with
you at night, to welcome the strange, uncoercive
incense of another day.

HIS SPEECH

He rode on in a blaze of learning.
The torment of dolts and some fatuous lingering—
inspired Haydn-like church thunders,
simple advents of shifting cultures.

The presences, schoolrooms and endeavors,
suffering—were the fires of crimson bells.
The blocked language that could unite nations
throbbed in his skull. No glory hymn,

but a crashed music, outpouring that
was intense. It was nothing, everything,
the very speech of our dust.

SPECIES TALK

Thinking back, we had a sweet mating,
copulation was not the residence
company, not the tightly scripted, but ascendingly
the occasional visitor. Or so it seemed.
Death at the end, mortal was not
the vulgar synonymous.

Appearances are deceiving, like
pelicans, ostriches.
We were separate partners, Kama Sutra evocations.
In lives, vertically known to conclude,
failed swimmers in some chronic
overwhelming sea.

Our courtship had the grace of
infidelities, myriad moods—
so many skies. And that soul confrontation,
such strange unwed carnal thoughts, seeds,
regeneration, mixed with sometimes
darling celibacy.

YOU THINK THAT

You think that "being sad" you are
sympathetic to somebody dying;
you are mistaken. Death is not like wearing an
overcoat, or using a Xerox. But the narrow-ledged
besieged universe, with a crack-up for all,
no familiars—will blow
your head off.

You think death is a nostalgic passivity;
wrong. No comparison, a war of so much individuality,
every stammer is a statement; an existence so
terribly cogent, you'll not go near.
Unless you are caring into
the Fire. Descending, and holding that dear

immensity of his life, so
unforbidding in itself,
you can die too.

THE BEACON

En route to the Cape, the cranberry factory
was a beacon. Acid sweetness to mind,
sandy terrain and the red painted berries advertised
on plank fences. You driving, and watching for
turns. Crouched by your side, I imbibed
the little country stop lights.

Did I know paradise by the signs?
The Ocean Spray industry, located at some sleepy
old town, featuring ceramics and fruit. Like
rose petals in my head, the strewn gift of equilibrium was
part of the experience soul-perfect.
Stacks of the cans and jars,

jelly and juices, creating mundane images
so blessed. Did I know I'd remember
the visionary passages? You, shifting the ancient Buick
into neutral. No time for derision, though
actuality recalled is a butterfly fed
to Cruelty. Miles of

sand and sea, and the first sight of it
was CRANBERRY. Such a discreet factory, like the first
signs of love. Where all journeys begin and
surely don't end. But later our lives broke down
and the flashback like a beacon, in
that ambered placement.

THE FORBIDDEN

Awful, not to be sleeping in
the same bed with you. The respectability
of medical opinion, that destroys not
just hope, but the actual network of pleasure we
built in life. Never again, the sane encounter—
and the undercover hint of form,
the plasticity of companionship that nobody
mentions. Nightly conjunctions, part

dreams, the ceiling blink of cars from outside
on the country road. The low scatter, and grace-pattering
rain, color of consciousness. That we are
more than individuals. And now rent,
kept apart, not by warring theatrical families,
but by doctors and syringes.

In their distant birdcage, taking
account. Ravenously, I look forward to even
the skimpiest meeting allowed, and our unrealistic
true love. Unfettered and determined
like headlights on a road.

PAEAN

In the grip of heavy medication and physical pain,
he kept open mind and identity.
Notaries at the scene can't transmit
to the observer the extent,
and heroism.

Friends and onlookers had no stomach
for the severe treatment to their nerves—when
they heard him gag and choke on the respiratory machine,
they stopped their ears. He was
grappling with

the crucifixion of dying. Not even
doctors or poets were equipped to see the courage
and congestion, as if the body were a whole
city, in surges of wisdom and tragic scrutiny. Between
bouts of morphine and enforced

daze, he was steady. As well maintaining
desire in the corrosion of hospitals.
Thus counselors (protected by the rind of comic
distance) said, "Nothing's that serious."
No doctrine or bias can give

the glory to him. That from every portal,
the humble unreduced light outside, putting to flight
all generalities, siphoning the sun; the room,
his consciousness, I'll break
my mind to tell of.

STURDY TRUTH IN A RARIFIED FOG

The way it has turned out since you
died, raging in face of the crisis I cleave
to our relation—my only reality.
The tentative glitter

between us didn't begin yesterday.
Mauve dawn stirring on rooftops,
the bronze tiered water towers—
a temerity-softened

coming of light. The dusky shambles, morning was
the path of our long life together.
Until the system spread, your
singular beloved person I

only half discerned. In today's perversity
analyses, who wants to expose love?
Memories slide by, tiny entries left
ajar. Like when we

noticed in autumn the dropped
leaves scudding under
parked cars.

UNTITLED

The closest thing I can remember
about your kiss, it was like a breeze.
I blanked out when you got close,
it was sensual, it was not sensual,

no compromise or plan.
A whorled, airy unintention, some
nowhere of the softest passing through,
like a window opening.

I can't remember lips,
but felt them
cool and warm, untitled
like a breeze.

FLESH AND NATURE

Your fingertips were the chromosome that
naturalists state they obtain
from petals and flowers,

and the holiness thereof.
Representative, prehistoric—
the improvised heirs of a quiet flesh.

Like tender prayers, their grasp
linked to certitude. I stood among godliness, to
your stem united.

Our love was whole and personal,
no marked place separated, as virginity
is to the life span.

And death, not the consummation
of us. Your handclasp enlightened
like the nature of flowers

reflected some principle.
Our joy was Eden.
But when you died, it was insane.

And nature didn't save us,
this wide-eyed grief
stalk.

THE TREE OF NECESSITY

It was his overload tree. Out of
necessity, he let the branches expend,

too wild. Thick soil, moss-fouled,
ringed skinny trunk, bending

tough in the unwatered heat.
An old-age brownish glare not wiped

out, the inner resplendent.
All things to the soul that bore it.

Like a pile of poems, and the love
he gave to the tippled leaves,

growing where the sun goes,
in spite of him.

THE SHELTER

The ingredients aren't feminism,
or the male frippery of
protecting the little lady, or that
shoddy show of putting women at
a weak disadvantage.

But I felt in my bones how you
always guarded me.
Now you've left this life, I'm unguarded.
The interchange of vigilance we
kept going, maybe in

the same tiger way. Like some
chivalry, barbed guarantee.
But not spotlighted either, taking
care of each other. Not for
amused company either.

But like one night on Eighth Street, a bunch,
drug juveniles elbowed me, in front of a shoe store—
rape and robbery leaked out of
their teeth-fillings, you came up and
broke it up.

We bounced off their clichés.
The petty violence, like a colorful
truck wreck. Like baleful landlords, and stupid
relatives, nasty ineptitudes lurking under
the gauche deceits of mankind

(you disconnected from, in
the mysterious wires of your integrity).
Now, yourself wrested from our long
life. I am physically bleeding, not by gender
or age, and it has nothing

to do with anything but your absence.
In some fair countenance of our love, we
were always staving off outside
attack. When you were in
the Army, I worried myself crazy—

sheltering the two thousand centuries
of each other. And boils down to the limits,
like numbers. Part of the nuptials, and strenuously
sanctuary. Don't ask why, it
was absolutely simple.

EARLY SPRING

The clouds are pink, a syntax of spring.
Old bereaved women weeping at the window boxes
about what more they might have done, watering
the luscious tulip bulbs with penitence.

An early spring. Suburbia reigns,
docile and forgiving, showing pansies'
velvet crisis. Opposing counterfeit, and lilies
of the valley dally fragrances.

By some sympathetic alliance,
a flash before the boom, sunshine and rain.
Greenleaf quotes cohesion, with enough discord
for blossoming through.

WHY A CORNER IN THE APARTMENT
PUTS ME TO SLEEP

This corner makes me drowsy
like a bad unguent. Your absence is
a need to close my eyes. The cracked Tiffany lamp
a shaded rose, you bought at a Brooklyn thrift shop—
now a throbbed Persephone
gone underground.

You are no epitaph but that scarred piano
we used to play. Great music trivializes, when
so much worse hurts, can't keep my
eyelids open. The hypnotizing rugs that
stare into Alone. My thoughts sway into violent,
black somnambulent, cold death

supplying the madness of your gone.
Don't let me dream, doze and deny, like
a TV slob. Avenues across the room, so dear,
the places where you were, the very
chairs excluding welcome.
And the multitudes

that held us, all withdrawn.
Hey quick! I've got to stand up,
fighting off sleep, not the better for
waking.

LOVE IS

Love is not gourmet
cream truffles
or pacified sucks.

But walking on broken rocks
where nobody goes—
love is.

THE SUPERSTITION

Seeing a snapshot of you,
I thought your hands were my hands.
You were about to open a book,
your reading glasses at the hollow of a
knuckle, raised veins and the pinched elongations
of age. And that my

breath devoured the scope of them.
The lithe geography and contour of your fingers.
Who could make fun of age?
but a mind drenched in funland,
laughing like newspapers at cripples.
I'm pleased your wrist is

the replica of my bones.
Though yours are more favored, the whip-edge of
purpose, in their quiet handsomeness.
When I could no longer clasp of you the warmth,
I became in my avarice (that you'd died)
the very dogma of comparison.

One flesh, one person.
Your hands are me.
To outsiders, this could sound
like superstition. The sacred thrust between us,
too late renewed.

I am jealous of my love for you,
thrillingly, the incest excitement catches
me adrift. I am a tree
hit by lightning.
It is natural to love you,
I am the slave of my ardor, nobody
knows your quality as I, who
sprang to your need.

But your death is no excuse
for my lax thinking. You who disappeared
into death's fantasy—must I
blame myself, too much the speaking vessel?
Of your guilelessness, good works and the trust,
sex undeciphered, halves
to the brain . . . Our days were the silky ladders
I hallow and climb, most frail
entity. And I retaliate against

the ideal set for me,
that can't help you now. My plundered
adoration is unworthy, I am a
child compared to the chalice of understanding,
the greening boughs and grown-up joys and griefs,
look back to our exchanged messages, when love
itself was an outcry for strength.
And the meaninglessness that makes
words into ashes; I can't

distance myself from you, and will
never want to.

THE GUESS

He was learning so much from
his last illness, it was almost unbearable.
The wisdom of his body had been surfeit, the sinews
in an oak. And love was
at the roots.

And he guessed all men were
saviors—his hands extended to
the world his gratitude. And they seemed
empty, the fullness
invisible.

LESLIE'S GLANCE

How close you appeared to your
stealthy critics. In a silence, you didn't
load up on any suspicion. They thought you were
naïve, or their best friend.

The look you gave, undirected; that
went lengths. Cast back, as on a still river,
the deep embankment; I've seen you, not
even studiously, studying.

As if at one with your deceivers.
No, you skimmed their vices in the deep
of utter patience. And strongholds
only assisted by calm.

Assurances so unintended—in
your eyes, they saw nothing
but themselves.

PAINKILLER

Ardent work is a painkiller,
like just your handwriting on a page,
and doing mathematics—that connects with central
neurological tracks, vast circulatory blood-

lights, into aphrodisiacal
forgetfulness. And the more aching a line
of poem, the more it lulls.
Intense dancers on broken toes

insist they never noticed. Like Tchaikovsky
using his tears on laboring music scores, the
melody narcotic. Or running the good
race eludes the hurt.

Mind over matter? It's the brandy gift
of life. Or from a crack in Nothingness—
creation of the world. And must have
been some backbreaking,

godless job. Enormous, long time
over-hours. Working like a dog, that
sweet analgesic postponement
of the End.

The impact is simmering down, as into
a solvent liquid. That I'll never hear your voice
again, but through a medium like
rain. Or will see you but in a lightning flash.
You are nature's speech, the young girth
and deadly imprint.

I eagerly wait the date of your rebirth, in
the endless window-sky. Hovering cloud, really a
gilded shadow that lights your face outline. Waters
and land permit no elegy translated.
But a stark villanelle, facts rendered.
An indefinite, glorious seeding,

the element that draws us closest. Nucleus of
a meadow, the grass-tips' ghost your
being. Bend me to earth, the only hereafter after death.
O shades beneath the sun. Or I don't understand it—
like embracing a mystery hole in our minds,
this complex, heartbreak survival.

AT A RECENT CINEMA

GOD is bottomless as self-analysis.
The more guilt or profit, we
adhere to Glory.

Tears falling at a recent cinema
that happened to be real.
And dark shining words,

more talented than anything, we
ever learned before. About
our care-giving selves.

We tried
to save the world. But things turned out
as if we'd failed at

some church step. Because it
was real, we didn't
fail.

THE COMB

Certain mornings, I breathe in and kiss
your comb I've kept, a brown
celluloid you had.
Waiting in the atmosphere, a friendly warmth.
Epidermal, phenomenal, fantasia,

wool, silk, touch, headgear,
your hair. When the sun comes up,
I go to the bedroom where
I left your old comb, like a
last cohabitation.

And closer than photographs
to you, I can't speak of death, the morbidity
not to be understood by comforters,
their bottled tears and laughter
if I told them.

Like a Faulkner rose, in
all extremes. Momentarily vanquished
by our comb you used to use every
day. Communicating, wielding,
all I have of you.

And in the eye of civility, certainly
not the way to be. The old celluloid type,
the comb's manufactured amber
light pressed to my lips, like an
unconsummated wafer.

EASTER MUSIC

It slipped in the quiet of your flesh,
hand to your self, the phallic
kingdoms, private sanguinity, sexual arousal,
I knew I was in the presence, erotic.
My lifelong companion,
for you there was no one else to
tell your deathside.

You said, "Did I do harm? I hesitate
touching myself like it, was
it bad for the health?"
Quest, not irony, telling this almost
refuses language.
"My love—" I did not speak this
aloud, the mirage of touching
body to a tree,

I merged in the grip of blood
and salt, "all acts are fair as death
reaches you. Let masturbation flow
through your body as to
a thirsty bible."

GRIEF

My tears are falling like into
an old railroad depot sink,
in a public rest room. Nobody there, the
battered enamel and swinging door stalls, the citadel
of derelict gradings.

And the ravage continues, night and days
with memories so travelled—to a dim bulb's
desecration. Cold grips the guts of
those who'd secrete their
grief.

To adorn the bitterness and shame
that death could kill us.
My hope remains, like those gray paper towels
stuffed in a basket. Panic-images crowd
revoked space,

your full worth strikes me blindly,
I grope for the fragments. Where do people go
to get away? to throw-up or succumb. Their
belligerent sobs echoing in some degenerate privacy,
a last redoubt, in this

forgotten, marble run-down place.
And the remorseless, invective truisms,
drip, drip, scalding from
their eyes, like a
broken faucet.

INADVERTENT

My uncle was a weakling and a crook;
he cheated and lied, and left
a trail of disoriented lives, children and wives.
A wastrel. But sheerly by inadvertence, he
did something right, and put up a green awning at the front
of his house, that I doted
on, as a child.

In our small-town neighborhood, it stood out.
No follow-up; years later I'm in New York,
and grief is at my throat, an occurrence so bitter,
the death of someone closer to me than life—
and nothing is left but my paralysis of
will, and helplessness.

Across the street I see an old apartment; and an
unlikely, ruffled awning (this one is brown)
flapping at a window.
And, voluptuous hope sweats my dreams; light-dews of
memory, as if something by chance was
bearable and restorative.

Inadvertent, accidental, self-deluding. Against
the terrible and agonized death, that won't
be canceled. Why do I keep looking at a flapping
awning? and not even about
my uncle.

JINGLE DREAM

Even if in my dream, by your death
you were leaving me, I want
to go back and envisage each moment,
the hunch of your shoulders like
a coal miner in a cave,

and the desperate leaving face,
and tears of rejection
against me, that you wanted
to go. I want to go back
to my misery,

that you were leaving.
Because you were
still there in
my dream.

NAME

I want to hear myself saying your
name. Friends think I'm one-pronged, hanging
every vessel and frond on some memorial
standard. After a decent interval,
when everybody pretends it

doesn't matter. To me, heart-sage,
the greening location of your secret essence.
Incoherence on the brink of how
much I need you. The greatest discovery
that evokes a live presence

to my discernments.
Sprouts from a shrub.
I tawdrily bring you into the conversation
whenever I can.

Want to fill up on your name,
thoughts cup into it.
The residual echoing.

OCCUPANCY

My self was interrupted by
grief, as a book cover is interrupted
by inside pages, as a structure
by sacred occupancy, the vanishing—
your face. My self,

interrupted by the knowledge of
abyss. I hugged the nearness, your body's
still warm, total, swerving,
disobedient to all limits,
rich, uncharted

physicality.

PIGEON WINGS

Going through to the healing ingredient—
the sound of pigeon wings.
You've been lost in death for two years, and I
can no longer hold you away from it.
Today, some pigeons' liftoff
from the fire escape,

feather and bone rufflings.
Their windy pinions are nearly better than
a slug of alcohol, or physically
tantamount. My damned, indrawn denials, not
wanting a curative, when there's no cure.
Their swatchy, airborne

pigeon-thick flesh, like a pile
of dirt be my master. These dumb elders of
the sky, burnt candles szzing.
The ashes of alive, eavesdropping from
above. And only the pillows
of their flight rest me.

RESTORATION OF TRUST

Restoration of trust is an almost
visible change, like attitudes
being a sharp alteration in
weather; I see the lapses' irony,
seer wrong predicted
here into love's relief.

The reward of odd angels: the young woman who
found my husband's mother's inheritance
only gift of real pearls and her also finding his lost
wedding ring. The insignia inside the band,
the gold-written date of our
marriage day, June 4th.

The twinned return of what is
now my only savored entry. Blessing
on the callow sophistication,
my side that can be shocked,
but in the realization I
can still be touched.

What good the value pearls, and size of the ring?
But I can still see the shelves
and feel the organization of
warmth and loyalty where we
both worked, and his death
I can still vehemently
deny.

RENEWED HOPE

Renewed hope, that's all,
a prosaic underbreath
plain as paper.

Your body, my life's
spilled day, where darkness
was evaporating.

I grasp at the foolish conundrum, that
you are still downstairs,
at home in our house.

Reconstructed from oblivion. I
keep listening for footsteps
and thoughts.

SERENADE

Every change in the weather is that you are
not here to feel it. No hands cup
the cup. Your coat hangers hang empty in the closet,
the death-ride has carried you;
psychologists and friends may survey the wreckage and cringe,
fitting their ideas on your demise as fitting.
But they don't know what you
are missing.

The grand willingness you lived for,
gestures of unseen faith.
Tonight, the moon's heavy rising languor over a Village bar,
you will not register in your mind.
The moon, liquidity and mists, staggering between
buildings, foggy and graceful. Like the last time we saw
Balanchine's *Serenade* at the State Theater,
the equivalent, his absorption.

The world you'd embarked on, that waited for
a tryst, the blue-lit, elegiac costumes, sparse scenery
nobody had to explain. How silently you scanned it,
the moon-tulle dancer swaying in the mist,
the tactile and rough awareness—and all your consciousness
of it, terminated.

People don't want to think that's what happens.
Even art's great disposition, like a
kiss, forever denied you. Refracted energy, shimmering
like an aura alongside buildings; the very
idea of obliteration itself,
snuffed out.

TWILIGHT RAIN

Wind-splashed, hesitant on the window,
its own hesitant rhythm, I live in the conch
almost invisible to the ear.
Rain-doodlings like the faulty radiator drip at
the heart of things.

Your life taken away from me, as from
under a magician's sheet;
I have vanished in rain, into the waterspouts I
hear, the whispering hairline-drizzle.
Don't disguise the comfort

I crave. Forcibly disowned, the once radiant lamps
still in this room, the twilight shift.
How can I describe what's lost, when you are the loss?
Nothing left but the sporadic detail,
unpredictably crusaders

of reality, these drops of
fresh water. Linking yet to the cause
of you. Like particles delayed, bits of light-show
memory, I cling to.

UNTITLED 2

Your death awakened me from
the death sleep of most of my life,
woke me from dodging the missiles, now I'm
letting them fall on.

Sitting upright, when I used
to crawl under adages and excuses.
Too late I saw the causal glories, I
take off my shield.

Your death that awaited, called me
out of all postponements.
Like a birth, leaving the general run of
my life, the sophist entertainment

of playing the crowd.
Alive with your vanished heartbeat,
I see where I missed the mission.
It's the beginning of action

too late, I step into the door of light
where our seedling youth and maturity
were actually quiescent. Now death
tells me to match the flower.

POLLY'S LEGACY

Now the place has been sold, from our
home and the scamper moss,
and the joy on the walls, and the many
signs of individual, not measured
by tithes and doubt, and colored glass vases
and ruin, but hearts and seamed
obscure parts, I asked Polly
what wooden and gold
treasures she would like from us,
from Leslie and me, what chair
or drinking glass, what
piano key, what soft African pillow,
what old TV tuner or rug,

what do you want, Polly
of our vast assembled heartbreak treasures,
what fireplace irons, what sailboat or skis, or pencil
or books, every eye you cast on our full life is at your service,
you are the heir of ages and edges that made
sense, beds and stairs, and bundles of
stars, I could leave to you blankets,
white silk, or where we buttered biscuits
you say in return, "I want only one night of
the memory, you and Leslie at the table, and Ben Weber
playing 'The Old Rugged Cross,' so passionately
on the foot pedal organ, he broke it.
I only want the dialogue, not even
any word like love can encompass."
The bright season of night
for which mortality is headed,
where we are now.
Jane, you said, give memories
high beam, in high grass,
on Grand Avenue, where people still

had names in Saratoga's secret
state of mind where bitterroot pleasure had its
Benjamin Franklin stove, and realm, before
so much had perished.

And yes cried her answer
and nothing yelled
possessions but appropriate
and opposed to the jaws of
collecting, the one rare spot that friendship
embraced. That braced and sang,
the long nights fell endlessly, grouped
around the table, I leave for you
unexplained. The vision outside,
the old house we lived in,
the way we spent our life. The breath
exchanged, I pass on freely,
our treasure of trust
and grain somewhere the plan before
anyone died, my memorial gift
of days passed on.
Ben crashing notes on the organ
the local witnesses of one
summer night, belongs
always to you.